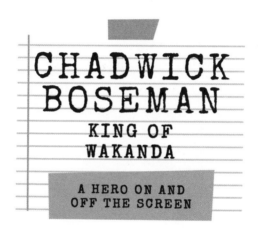

CHADWICK BOSEMAN

KING OF WAKANDA

A HERO ON AND OFF THE SCREEN

Published by Bushel & Peck Books, a family-run publishing house in Fresno, California, that believes in uplifting children with the highest standards of art, music, literature, and ideas. Find beautiful books for gifted young minds at www.bushelandpeckbooks.com.

Type set in LTC Kennerley Pro, Special Elite, Nexa Rust Sans, Josefin Sans, and AltaCalifornia.

Bushel & Peck Books is dedicated to fighting illiteracy all over the world. For every book we sell, we donate one to a child in need—book for book. To nominate a school or organization to receive free books, please visit www.bushelandpeckbooks.com.

LCCN: 2023951181

ISBN: 978-1-63819-177-3

First Edition

Printed in China

1 3 5 7 9 10 8 6 4 2

BLACK HISTORY HEROES

CHRIS
SINGLETON
WITH RYAN G.
VAN CLEAVE

ILLUSTRATED BY
ADRIANA
PÉREZ
PERALES

CHADWICK BOSEMAN

KING OF WAKANDA

A HERO ON AND
OFF THE SCREEN

MILK +
COOKIES

Contents

Dedicated to the memory of the
victims of the Mother Emanuel
Church Tragedy:

REV. SHARONDA COLEMAN-SINGLETON
REV. CLEMENTA PINCKNEY
CYNTHIA GRAHAM HURD
SUSIE JACKSON
ETHEL LANCE
REV. DEPAYNE MIDDLETON-DOCTOR
TYWANZA SANDERS
REV. DANIEL SIMMONS
MYRA THOMPSON
& SURVIVORS

1

An Epic Introduction: Meet Chadwick!

When it comes down to it, I'd rather have an
action figure than a Golden Globe.

—CHADWICK BOSEMAN

Picture this: it's the premiere night of *Black Panther*. Marvel Studios spent $200 million to make a movie about Black Panther and his homeland, Wakanda—a futuristic African nation that featured spaceships, skyscrapers, and a near-endless array of amazing costumes.

Everyone knew the Black Panther character stole the show in the 2016 Marvel film *Captain America: Civil War*. Could that same character lead Marvel to another smash hit two years later? Was the world ready for a Black main character in a superhero movie? Or a superhero film largely created by a team of Black filmmakers, including 31-year-old Ryan Coogler, the first African American director of a Marvel movie?

Fans are decked out in Wakanda-inspired outfits, and the red carpet teems with celebs. Everyone's eyes are glued to one person—the King of Wakanda himself, the actor Chadwick Boseman.

You might know him as T'Challa, but Chadwick was a real-life superhero, too. He made the world a better place with his acting skills, generosity, and dedication to making a difference.

Born and raised in South Carolina, Chadwick was just a regular kid with big dreams. His journey began in the hallways of his high school, where he starred in plays and got involved in a theater program. But that's just the beginning.

He went on to study at prestigious acting institutions where he **honed** his ability to write, direct, and act.

Like so many people do when they chase a big dream, Chadwick struggled. Even in the toughest moments, Chadwick refused to quit. "Whatever you choose for a career path, remember the struggles along the way are only meant to shape you for your purpose." And his purpose was to share important stories—especially African American stories—with the world.

People first took notice of Chadwick's acting ability when he accepted the role of legendary baseball player Jackie Robinson in the film *42*. From that moment on, he continued to wow audiences by bringing powerful stories to life. But it was his role as T'Challa, the Black Panther, that turned him into a global superstar.

Chadwick's impact went way beyond cool action scenes and box office records. *Black Panther* was a game changer. It was a commercially successful, critically acclaimed film that celebrated

Black culture, power, and strength. It showed the world that superheroes come in all colors and that representation matters. As Chadwick once said, "When you play characters, you shouldn't just be putting on their characteristics—you should be finding it inside yourself."

And he did just that.

Black Panther wasn't Chadwick's only important film, however. He also portrayed other iconic figures like musician James Brown, the "Godfather of Soul," in *Get on Up* and Thurgood Marshall, the first Black Supreme Court Justice, in *Marshall*. Through these roles, Chadwick brought the stories of Black trailblazers and heroes to the big screen, inspiring millions around the globe.

Now, you might be thinking, "Okay, Chadwick was an amazing actor, but what about offscreen?" To put it plainly, he was equally incredible. Chadwick used his fame and fortune to make a real difference. He supported charities, visited sick kids in hospitals, and worked to empower young people to follow their dreams. Through and through, he was a true **humanitarian**.

One of Chadwick's most memorable moments was when he surprised Black Panther fans on *The Tonight Show with Jimmy Fallon*. The fans thought they were just recording video messages

to thank Chadwick for his incredible work, but little did they know that he was hiding behind a curtain, ready to give them the surprise of a lifetime. The smiles and tears of joy on their faces when he appeared were beyond measure. Moments like this show just how much Chadwick cared about his fans and the impact he had on their lives.

But even superheroes must face their own battles. In 2020, the world was shocked to learn that Chadwick had been privately fighting colon cancer for four years. Despite his illness, he continued to work on films and engage in **philanthropy**. He showed us that no matter what life throws at us, we can be strong and resilient and keep pushing forward.

Sadly, Chadwick Boseman passed away on August 28, 2020, but his legacy lives on. He left a lasting impact on the world, not only through his work on the big screen but also through the kindness and inspiration he spread off-screen. Today, people of all ages still cross their arms in the Wakanda **salute**, honoring the memory of a hero who taught us the power of storytelling, representation, and making a difference.

So, as we embark on this journey through Chadwick's life, let's remember the wise words of T'Challa himself: "In times of crisis, the wise build bridges, while the foolish build barriers." Chadwick Boseman was a bridge-builder, connecting people through his talent, passion, and love for humanity. Now, it's time to dive deeper into the incredible life and legacy of the one and only Chadwick Boseman—a hero both on and off the screen.

WORDS TO KNOW

honed: To make something, like a skill or talent, better and sharper through lots of hard practice or work.

humanitarian: A person who is dedicated to improving the lives of others, often through actions such as providing aid and support or advocating for human rights.

philanthropy: The act of giving time, money, or help to others, especially to make the world a better place.

salute: A gesture of respect, usually done by raising a hand to the forehead.

THE WORLD AT THE TIME

In 2016:

- The augmented reality game, *Pokémon Go,* becomes a cultural phenomenon.
- *Deadpool* is one of the biggest film hits of the year.
- After 108 years, the Chicago Cubs win the World Series.

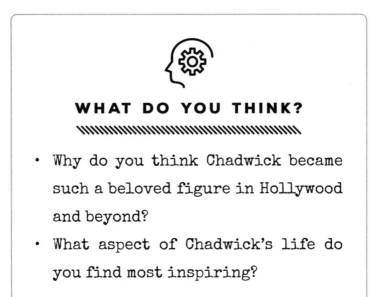

WHAT DO YOU THINK?

- Why do you think Chadwick became such a beloved figure in Hollywood and beyond?
- What aspect of Chadwick's life do you find most inspiring?

2

The Origin Story: From Small-Town Kid to Big-Time Dreamer

As an African American actor, a lot of our stories haven't been told.

—CHADWICK BOSEMAN

So, what's the origin story of our hero, Chadwick Aaron Boseman? Like so many of the best tales, it starts with a child who has an important dream.

Born on November 29, 1976, Chadwick grew up in a loving, close-knit Christian family from Anderson, South Carolina. His dad, Leroy, worked at a textile factory and had a side business as a furniture upholsterer, while his mom, Carolyn, was a nurse. They taught Chadwick the importance of hard work, dedication, and chasing his dreams. And let's not forget about his two siblings—his eldest brother, Derrick, a future preacher, and middle brother, Kevin, a dancer. Each boy was five years apart from the others, but they were close, so his older brothers had a lot of influence on their youngest brother.

Chadwick was a quiet kid who belonged to a local choir and youth group, and he loved to play sports, practice martial arts, and draw. "Maybe one day," he sometimes thought, "I'll become an architect."

Growing up, Chadwick's house was always filled with laughter, music, and the aroma of his

mom's homemade Southern cooking. Imagine the mouthwatering scent of cornbread, macaroni and cheese, and sweet Carolina BBQ wafting through the air as his family gathered around the table, sharing stories of their day. It was in these moments that Chadwick learned the power of storytelling and how it could bring people together.

His childhood wasn't without challenges, however.

Racism was the norm for South Carolina during this time. His school district even remained

segregated until just before Chadwick was born. Small wonder then that Chadwick and his friends got yelled at and called names just for walking down the street. At one point, someone in a car even chased him.

Yet Chadwick didn't let racism stop him from pursuing his dream, which had become being

a professional basketball player. By the time he attended T. L. Hanna High School, he was a star player. Good enough, in fact, that colleges came to recruit him. One of his proudest sports moments was playing against future NBA Hall of Famer Kevin Garnett. "I didn't match up with him, but I scored on him," Chadwick recalled years later on *Jimmy Kimmel Live*. "I did an up and under on him."

Then another challenge emerged.

During Chadwick's junior year of high school, one of his friends on the basketball team was shot and killed. To cope with the crushing sadness and honor his friend's life, Chadwick wrote a play entitled *Crossroads* and staged a performance at the high school.

This experience proved to be transformative. "I just had a feeling that this was something that was calling me," he said in a later *Rolling Stone* interview. "Suddenly, basketball wasn't as important."

It was a turning point in his life, showing Chadwick that he could use his talents to make a

difference and heal others. He still played varsity basketball for the rest of his time in high school, and he participated in track and field as well as the speech and debate team, but he spent all the time he could in the drama department, just as his brother Kevin had done.

THIS was Chadwick's future.

Through it all, Chadwick's family was his rock, cheering him on from the sidelines and always believing in his dreams. When he decided to pursue acting as a career, they were right there, offering endless support and encouragement. His family's love was the fuel that ignited his unstoppable drive.

WORDS TO KNOW

segregation: The practice of separating people based on factors such as race, gender, or religion; often used to discuss the forced separation of different racial groups.

THE WORLD AT THE TIME

In 1992:

- Disney releases *Aladdin,* and the animated film is a huge success.
- the Super Nintendo Entertainment System (SNES) becomes popular among kids, with games like *The Legend of Zelda: A Link to the Past* and *Super Mario Kart.*
- the Cartoon Network begins, providing a dedicated channel for animated TV shows and movies.

WHAT DO YOU THINK?

- How did Chadwick's childhood experiences contribute to his later success in acting?

- If you could meet Chadwick's family, what would you ask them about his life?

3

The Adventure Begins: A Passion for Performing

The only difference between a hero and a villain is that the villain chooses to use that power in a way that is selfish and hurts other people.

—CHADWICK BOSEMAN

The next step of Chadwick's journey was to attend Howard University, a school known to many as "The **Mecca**" because of its awesome history as a historically Black college and its commitment to producing influential African American leaders in all fields of study. Nestled in the heart of Washington, DC, it was the perfect place for our hero to spread his wings and soar to new heights.

Though we think of Chadwick as a major Hollywood actor, at that time, he was a student who focused his efforts on plays and the world of theater. He learned a lot about writing and acting while there, though his intension was to be a great director.

At Howard, Chadwick studied under some seriously amazing teachers. One of them was the incredible Al Freeman Jr., an actor and director who helped Chadwick unlock his full potential. Freeman pushed Chadwick to dig deep, find the truth in his performances, and bring his characters to life in a way that would resonate with audiences.

Perhaps no one at Howard played a bigger role in Chadwick's education than his acting teacher,

the actress Phylicia Rashad, a graduate herself of Howard. Best known for her role on the TV sitcom *The Cosby Show*, this **Emmy**-nominated and **Tony**-winning actress was named "The Mother of the Black Community" at the 2010 **NAACP** Image Awards.

"What I saw in him was the sky was the limit," Rashad said. "He never asked me to introduce him to anyone—that's not his way. He was going to make it on his own merits."

Chadwick's commitment to earn his way to the top was evident in all he did both in and out of the classroom. Sure, he was a hard worker who put in the long hours and effort to learn his craft, but he was already showing his true colors as a **change agent**. When the administrators at Howard decided to merge the College of Fine Arts into the College of Arts & Sciences, Chadwick led a peaceful protest because he worried that this action would water down the quality of education. The change still happened, but Chadwick took a stand for something he believed in—something he'd do again and again down the road.

Chadwick's education didn't stop at Howard. Thanks to the support and encouragement of his mentor Rashad, he scored a spot in the summer theater program at the acclaimed British American Drama Academy at Oxford University. You heard that right—our hero was about to go international, and he hadn't even completed his Bachelor of Fine Arts in Directing yet!

But he didn't have the funds to make it happen. Howard University was expensive, and Chadwick's family couldn't help him take advantage of this amazing opportunity.

Rashad, though, went the extra mile. She reached out to celebrity friends and found the funding so Chadwick and eight of his fellow classmates could take this exciting trip to England to take their acting skills to the next level.

It's easy to imagine the wide smile on Chadwick's face as he stepped off the plane in London, with the cool, damp air hitting his face and the iconic red double-decker buses zipping by. The city was a whirlwind of history, culture, and inspiration—the ideal place for Chadwick to continue his journey.

In that summer theater program, Chadwick studied alongside some of the best and brightest young actors from around the world. Together, they delved into the works of Shakespeare, explored the **nuances** of stagecraft, and pushed their boundaries as performers. A few years before, Chadwick was writing his first play, *Crossroads*, and now here he was, sitting in an old, stone-walled classroom with the sound of rain pattering against the window as he and his classmates dove into such classics as *Romeo and Juliet* and *Hamlet*.

Want to know how great this theater program is? Just consider a few of the other actors who attended it over the years: Orlando Bloom, Paul Rudd, David Schwimmer, Paul Giamatti, and now, Chadwick Boseman, too!

With his bags packed and his heart full of memories, Chadwick returned to the United States,

ready to put his newfound knowledge and skills to the test. He was more determined than ever to make his mark on the world of acting and share his unique voice with the world. It was time to take the world by storm!

Did Chadwick ever discover who the anonymous celebrity benefactor was? Absolutely. It was **Oscar-** and Tony-winning actor Denzel Washington.

Years later, Boseman gave a speech honoring Washington for a lifetime achievement award from the American Film Institute. "Imagine receiving the letter saying that your tuition for that summer was paid for and that your benefactor was none other than the dopest actor on the planet," Boseman said. "There is no Black Panther without Denzel Washington."

Gracious as always, Chadwick underplayed how his own unwavering determination and a fierce passion for his craft helped catapult him to superstardom. More on that in a moment!

WORDS TO KNOW

Mecca: A place that attracts a specific group of people due to its importance or significance, often used figuratively; also, the holiest city in Islam, located in Saudi Arabia.

Emmy: An award given annually for outstanding achievements in television, recognizing excellence in acting, directing, writing, and more.

Tony: An award given annually for outstanding achievements in live Broadway theater, recognizing excellence in acting, directing, writing, and more.

NAACP: The National Association for the Advancement of Colored People, a civil rights organization founded in 1909 to fight for the rights and equality of African Americans in the United States.

change agent: Someone who helps make big, positive changes happen, often by inspiring or leading others.

nuance: A subtle difference or distinction in meaning, opinion, or expression, often requiring careful attention to understand or appreciate fully.

Oscar: An award given annually for outstanding achievements in the film industry, recognizing excellence in acting, directing, writing, and more; presented by the Academy of Motion Picture Arts and Sciences.

THE WORLD AT THE TIME

In 2000:

- *Survivor* premieres on CBS, launching the reality TV craze.
- the first Harry Potter movie, *Harry Potter and the Sorcerer's Stone*, is released in theaters.
- the PlayStation 2 gaming console is launched, with popular games like *Gran Turismo 3* and *Final Fantasy X.*

WHAT DO YOU THINK?

- How important are early experiences in the arts for aspiring actors?
- How might a mentor help you pursue your own dreams and career?

4

Hustle and Heart: Enduring Adversity in the Big Apple

There's nothing more stressful than your stomach growling.

—CHADWICK BOSEMAN

New York City: the city that never sleeps and the place where dreams are made. Our hero, Chadwick Boseman, had his sights set on the Big Apple, ready to make a name for himself as a writer and director after his time at Howard University.

It was time to hustle!

Chadwick's move to the Bedford-Stuyvesant neighborhood of New York City was a bold leap. He once said, "You have to step out of the box. That's how you're going to find out who you really are, by stepping out of that comfort zone." And step out he did, embracing the bustling city life, the vibrant theater scene, and the competitive world of acting.

Chadwick spent a lot of time in coffee shops playing chess and writing plays. He also attended and graduated from the Digital Film Academy. The Director, who taught Chadwick's Acting for Directors class, said, "I remember his face and the level of concentration in his eyes. You could see internal processes working. At that time he was building himself. I could see he was putting the pieces together."

To help pay the bills, Chadwick taught acting lessons to kids at the Schomberg Center for Research in Black Culture in Harlem. He also wrote and directed a hip-hop play, *Deep Azure*, which was performed at the Congo Square Theatre Company in Chicago. In that play and other plays he wrote, Chadwick combined urban prose and poetry with a Shakespearean sensibility and style. There's his time in Oxford proving influential yet again.

And speaking of influence, this kind of mash-up of language, culture, and race was similar to what Lin Manuel Miranda later used to great effect with his 2015 smash hit, the musical *Hamilton*. Talk about being part of a great legacy!

Along the way, Chadwick took on some acting roles himself, but times were tough. New York City was extremely expensive to live in, and the writing/directing/acting business was full of so many talented people that it felt impossible to break through.

Three things helped Chadwick get through the most challenging times.

One—his brother, Kevin, whose dance career was quite literally reaching great new heights. Kevin went on to be a principal dancer for the prestigious Alvin Ailey American Dance Theater, and he danced for national tours of shows such as *The Lion King* and *Equus*. "My brother taught me how to dream," Boseman said.

Two—his father. "I saw him work a lot of third shifts, a lot of night shifts," Boseman explained. "Whenever I work a particularly hard week, I think of him."

Three—himself. He knew the only way to succeed was to persevere. "The industry looks for white actors and actresses, but it's not the same for Black actors. We have to really put the work in." So, he did.

Eventually, Chadwick started landing small but impactful roles on TV. He first appeared on TV in a 2003 episode of *Third Watch*, a popular police drama. In the same year, he scored a role in the long-running soap opera, *All My Children*, playing gang member Reggie Porter. Yet he was bothered by how the role leaned into Black stereotypes.

"I remember going home and thinking, 'Do I say something to them about this? Do I just do it?'" he wondered. "And I just couldn't do it. I had to voice my opinions and put my stamp on it."

I think there are some things we could improve with this character...

Even though this was his first significant acting credit, and the promised money would be welcome, he spoke up. For doing so, he was fired despite everyone saying he'd done a great job with his first week of filming. Even though the part was no longer his, the producers listened to his feedback and adjusted the role of Reggie Porter, making it less of a stereotype.

The replacement was 16-year-old Michael B. Jordan, a future film superstar who'd one day play the role of Erik Killmonger, the nemesis of Black Panther. How's that for a coincidence?

"Sometimes you need to get knocked down before you can really figure out what your fight is," Chadwick said. And boy, did he find his fight! Through the ups and downs of auditioning and dealing with the challenges of the industry, Chadwick's perseverance and self-belief carried him forward.

Chadwick knew that he had something special to offer, and the world was about to find out what that was.

THE WORLD AT THE TIME

In 2003:

- Apple's iTunes Music Store launches, revolutionizing the way people buy and listen to music.

- the beloved animated classic, Finding Nemo, is released by Pixar.
- *Call of Duty* releases, starting one of the most successful video game franchises of all time.

WHAT DO YOU THINK?

- As a member of the National Shakespeare Company of New York, Chadwick played Romeo in *Romeo and Juliet*. What other classic roles in theater or film would've been a great fit for him?
- How do you think Chadwick's time in New York shaped him as an actor?

Lights, Camera, Action! The Rise to Stardom

As soon as I came to LA, things immediately shifted for me. I was now actually here with the people who were making the decisions; I wasn't out in New York sending in tapes to LA.

—CHADWICK BOSEMAN

It's almost the perfect scene—Chadwick arriving in Los Angeles, the City of Angels, with palm trees swaying in the breeze and the sun shining bright. The air is filled with possibility, and Chadwick can feel it in his bones. THIS is where dreams come true. But before he can make it big, he's got to start somewhere, right?

Thanks to all his efforts in New York, TV producers began to recognize he had the ability to take on a serious acting role. In 2008, Chadwick's hard work began to really pay off—he landed a recurring role in the family drama series *Lincoln Heights*, where he played

Nathaniel "Nate" Ray Taylor. This opportunity allowed him to showcase his acting chops in a more significant way, but he wasn't done yet. In 2010, Chadwick debuted in the TV crime drama *Persons Unknown* as Sergeant McNair, proving that he could tackle a wide range of roles.

"The biggest thing about being an actor is to keep your imagination open, to keep yourself open, to what's possible," Chadwick said in an interview. That's exactly what he did, soaking up every experience and learning from each role. Every small success only fueled his desire to make a difference with his acting.

Chadwick's TV journey didn't stop there. In 2011, he made an appearance in the hit science-fiction show *Fringe*, followed by a guest role in the crime drama *Justified* in 2012. These roles were stepping stones, inching him closer to his dreams of Hollywood stardom.

One of Chadwick's most memorable TV roles came in 2013 when he starred as Graham McNair in the psychological drama about war crimes,

The Kill Hole. This role illustrated his incredible range and ability to captivate audiences, and Hollywood finally took notice.

That same year, Chadwick turned 35—fairly late for an actor to "make it"—and he earned the role of a lifetime, playing Jackie Robinson in the film *42*. This **biopic** told the inspiring story of the first African American to play in Major League Baseball, breaking barriers and changing the game forever.

Let's be clear, Chadwick was fit. He was "mostly **vegan**" and an avid juicer, plus he enjoyed sports and martial arts. But that's not the same as the type of grueling effort a professional athlete goes through daily. So, Chadwick hired a coach and trained five hours a day so he could properly portray Robinson on the screen. You'd think a high school jock like Chadwick would be a natural for this role, but he didn't know baseball all that well. He had to learn the sport inside and out, along with all the physical training!

"When you're doing a character you want to know the full landscape. You want to know them spiritually, mentally, and physically," he said. To that end he spoke with Robinson's wife for hours to ensure he understood things properly.

His portrayal of the emotional turmoil that Jackie Robinson felt earned Chadwick critical acclaim and put him on the map as a rising star. Audiences were captivated by his performance, and it was clear that this was just the beginning of his incredible journey.

As Chadwick's star continued to rise, he took on more and more challenging roles, proving that he was a force to be reckoned with in the world of film. In 2014, he played the Godfather of Soul, James Brown, in *Get On Up*. Chadwick dove headfirst into this part, mastering the iconic dance moves, learning to sing like the legend himself, and capturing the essence of James Brown's incredible spirit.

Just as he did with previous roles, Chadwick put himself through vigorous training so he could fully inhabit the role. Brown was as dynamic with his gritty, soulful singing as he was with his energetic, acrobatic dance moves. In short, the bar was high. Really high.

"I did the splits ninety-six times one day on *Get On Up*," Chadwick explained. Talk about a commitment!

It wasn't just biopics that showcased Chadwick's acting skills. He also acted in *Draft Day*, a sports film, and *Gods of Egypt*, an action film, flexing his muscles as a **bonafide** star. With each new role, Chadwick continued to prove that there was nothing he couldn't do.

So, what does this all mean for our hero? Well, it means that Chadwick was well on his way to superstardom. He had fought his way through the ranks, showcasing his enormous talent and dedication to his craft. By chasing his dreams and pushing the boundaries of what was possible, he'd captured the hearts and minds of audiences around the world, and it was clear that he was destined for greatness.

The next step in his career was a super leap forward—a multi-movie deal with Marvel Studios that paid him $700,00 for appearing in *Captain America: Civil War* and more than $2 million for *Black Panther*!

WORDS TO KNOW

biopic: A movie that tells the story of someone's life, usually about a famous or important person.

vegan: A person who does not eat or use animal products, including meat, dairy, eggs, and sometimes even honey; often for ethical, health, or environmental reasons.

bonafide: Genuine, authentic, or legitimate; often used to describe something or someone that is real, sincere, or truly qualified, without any deception or doubt.

THE WORLD AT THE TIME

In 2013:

- the "Harlem Shake" dance craze goes viral.
- Disney's *Frozen* is a massive hit in theaters, and "Let It Go" is sung by kids everywhere.
- *Grand Theft Auto V* breaks records and becomes one of the bestselling video games of all time.

WHAT DO YOU THINK?

- How did Chadwick's early acting experiences prepare him for his later, more prominent roles?
- What do you think was the turning point in Chadwick's early acting career?

6

King of Wakanda: The Black Panther Revolution

They can put the clothes on you,
but you've got to wear them.

—CHADWICK BOSEMAN

It's time to dive into the role that made Chadwick a household name and a true superhero in the eyes of millions—the one, the only, the incredible Black Panther!

It's 2016, and Chadwick has just been cast as T'Challa, a.k.a. Black Panther, in the Marvel Cinematic Universe (MCU). This is a big deal, people—like, HUGE. Not only is Black Panther the first Black superhero in mainstream comics, but this movie will be the first MCU film with a predominantly Black cast and crew. Talk about making history!

Even more surprising is that he wasn't asked to audition for the part. The Marvel Universe president simply called him up and offered him the gig because everyone knew—Chadwick was born for this role.

Fast forward to February 2018, and the world thrummed with excitement as *Black Panther* hit the big screen. Fans flocked to theaters, decked out in their finest Wakandan attire, ready to be transported to the technologically advanced, **Afrofuturistic** world of Wakanda. And let's be clear—they weren't disappointed.

The movie is a visual feast, filled with heart-pounding action, jaw-dropping special effects, and unforgettable characters. Chadwick's portrayal of T'Challa is nothing short of amazing. He's strong, wise, and compassionate—a true king and champion for the people of Wakanda.

Now, imagine yourself in the movie theater, the scent of popcorn filling the air as you watch

T'Challa face off against the villainous Killmonger, a Wakandan prince who trained his entire life so he could conquer Wakanda by right of challenge. Killmonger might be a villain, but he truly believes that his rebellion will make the world a better place. The tension is **palpable** as they battle for the fate of their nation, trading blows in an epic fight scene that leaves you on the edge of your seat.

But *Black Panther* isn't just about the action and special effects—it's also a powerful story about family, tradition, and the struggle to do what's right. Chadwick's T'Challa is a complex character, forced to navigate the challenges of leadership while grappling with his own doubts and fears. And that's what makes him so relatable and inspiring.

The cultural impact of *Black Panther* cannot be overstated. For the first time, millions of Black kids and adults saw a superhero who looked like them, a hero who celebrated their culture and heritage. The movie's message of unity, empow-

erment, and the importance of representation resonated with audiences around the world. It's also a necessary social commentary about racism, slavery, and poverty.

In Chadwick's own words, "It's a sea-change moment. I still remember the excitement people had seeing *Malcolm X*. And this is greater, because it includes other people, too. Everybody comes to see the Marvel movie."

Black Panther was more than just a movie—it was a movement, a celebration of Black excellence, and a powerful reminder that representation matters. The film went on to become a global phenomenon, earning over $1.3 billion at the box office and earning rave reviews from fans and critics alike. It also earned not one, not two, not three, but SEVEN Oscar nominations, including the big one: Best Picture.

Marvel Studios had never won an Oscar before, but thanks to Chadwick and Black Panther, it won three—Best Costume Design, Best Original Score, and Best Production Design.

Chadwick left an **indelible** mark on the world, breaking barriers and redefining what it meant to be a superhero. As T'Challa, the King of Wakanda, Chadwick showed audiences that heroes come in all colors. The impact of his portrayal was felt far beyond the movie screen, resonating with people of all ages and backgrounds.

"When I was a kid, I had no superhero that looked like me," Chadwick admitted. "I wanted to give kids an opportunity to see themselves on the screen." And he did just that. By bringing T'Challa to life, he inspired a new generation of kids to believe in their own power and potential.

WORDS TO KNOW

Afrofuturistic: A cultural and artistic movement that combines African history, traditions, and futuristic elements; often in science fiction and fantasy works.

palpable: Something that is so strong or clear that you can almost feel or touch it, like the excitement in a room before a big event.

indelible: Something that cannot be erased or removed; often referring to a lasting memory, impression, or mark.

THE WORLD AT THE TIME

In 2018:

- the InSight lander touches down on the surface of Mars.
- *Fortnite* captures the attention of millions of video gamers worldwide.
- "Baby Shark" becomes a viral music sensation.

WHAT DO YOU THINK?

- What impact do you think *Black Panther* has had on the superhero genre?

- DNA testing told Chadwick that some of his ancestors were Jola people from Guinea-Bissau, Krio people and Limba people from Sierra Leone, and Yoruba people from Nigeria. How important is it to know your ancestors? Have you ever considered using DNA testing to find out your family tree? If so, how did learning that make you feel?

7

Greatest Hits: Chadwick's Iconic Roles that Rocked Our World

I truly believe there's a truth that needs to enter the world at a particular time.

—CHADWICK BOSEMAN

We've seen him rise to stardom, and we've marveled at his iconic turn as Black Panther. But did you know that Chadwick's acting career didn't stop there? That's right! Our main man took on some other fantastic roles that made us laugh, cry, and cheer.

We already know that Chadwick had a knack for playing legendary African Americans like Jackie Robinson in 42 and James Brown in *Get On Up*. So, it wasn't a surprise that in 2017, he stepped into the shoes of another historical icon in the film *Marshall*. This courtroom drama told the story of Thurgood Marshall, the first Black Supreme Court Justice and another graduate of Howard University. His early career as a lawyer fighting for civil rights in the **Jim Crow** era was Hollywood worthy—no doubt about it.

While this film didn't require Chadwick to undergo training at the ballpark or in the gym, he still had to carefully plan and prepare. "It is the **Harlem Renaissance** and the **jazz era**, so although I didn't want to imitate what his voice might sound like or imitate his exact physicality, I did want to find the swagger or the rhythm of that time," he said. "So that is still very physical."

Even though Chadwick was born almost 70 years after Marshall, this story dealt with racism—something Chadwick knew from growing up in the South. "I know what it is to ride to school and have Confederate flags flying from trucks in front of me and behind me . . . I've been called 'boy' and every-thing else you could imag-ine." Channeling those painful experiences into this role made his acting memorable and powerful, despite most agreeing that the script itself was lacking. Even with that issue, many critics

recommended viewing the movie for Chadwick's acting alone.

Chadwick didn't just stick to biopics. He also took on roles in crime dramas like *21 Bridges*, where he played Andre Davis, an NYPD detec-

tive on the hunt for cop killers in the city that never sleeps. The intelligent, action-packed film had us on the edge of our seats, with Chadwick leading the charge as a determined and relentless hero.

It's worth noting that the original script had all the roles being played by white men. Chadwick encouraged changes to the story to address this, and that's how costar Sienna Miller got involved. And when her asking price was more than the producers wanted to pay, Chadwick donated some of his own salary to ensure she got what she deserved. He didn't just fight to support people of color—he worked just as hard to help women, too.

Another standout role for Chadwick came in the 2020 film *Da 5 Bloods*, directed by the legendary Black filmmaker Spike Lee. In this gripping drama, Chadwick played Stormin' Norman, the wise and charismatic leader of a group of Black Vietnam War veterans who return to the jungle years later to search for the remains of their fallen squad leader—and maybe, too, chase down a hidden stash of gold.

Chadwick's final role was in the film adaptation of August Wilson's play, *Ma Rainey's Black Bottom*, where he played Levee, an ambitious and talented trumpet player in Ma Rainey's band.

This **formidable** drama displayed Chadwick's ability to bring complex characters to life, earning him rave reviews and **posthumous** awards, including a Golden Globe for Best Actor.

As we look back on Chadwick's other memorable roles, it's clear that he was a true chameleon on-screen, able to transform himself into any character he took on. From historical figures to fictional heroes, Chadwick brought a level of depth, emotion, and nuance to each role that made his performances unforgettable.

And that's what makes Chadwick's story so inspiring—his passion for storytelling, his unwavering dedication to his craft, and his ability to touch the hearts of audiences around the world. These roles not only demonstrate his incredible talent but also serve as a testament to his legacy as an actor and a trailblazer in the industry.

💬

WORDS TO KNOW

Jim Crow: A term referring to the racist laws and policies in the United States that enforced racial segregation and limited the rights of African Americans, mostly in the South, from the late 1800s to the mid-1900s.

Harlem Renaissance: A time in the 1920s and 1930s when African American artists, writers, and musicians created lots of amazing new art, music, and literature in a neighborhood called Harlem in New York City.

jazz era (Jazz Age): A time during the 1920s when jazz music was very popular, and people loved to dance and have fun.

formidable: Something or someone that is very powerful and impressive, making it hard to compete with or overcome.

posthumous: Something that occurs or is awarded after a person's death, such as a book being published or an award being given.

THE WORLD AT THE TIME

In 2017:

- Nintendo releases the Switch gaming console, which features hit games like *The Legend of Zelda: Breath of the Wild* and *Super Mario Odyssey.*
- the TV show *Stranger Things* becomes a smash hit.
- fidget spinners are a must-have toy, providing stress relief and entertainment for kids.

WHAT DO YOU THINK?

\\

- Chadwick turned down the chance to play R&B music legend Sam Cooke because he didn't want to be type-cast as a biographical actor. What do you think about that decision?

- If you were an actor, would you prefer to play the roles of real-life people or fictional characters? Why?

8

Superhero Status: A Heart of Gold Off-Screen

I feel that I'm living my purpose. But the thing about purpose is that it unfolds to you more and more every day.

—CHADWICK BOSEMAN

Chadwick wasn't just an amazing actor—he was also an extraordinary humanitarian who cared deeply about making the world a better place. So, get ready to be inspired as we dive into the heartwarming world of Chadwick's philanthropy and community involvement!

Chadwick believed in the power of helping others and giving back to the community. One of the many ways he did this was by supporting organizations that provided opportunities and resources to young people, especially those from underprivileged backgrounds. He was passionate about empowering the next generation and helping them reach their full potential.

One such organization that Chadwick supported was the Boys & Girls Clubs of America. Chadwick even visited the club in his hometown of Anderson, South Carolina, where he spent time with the kids, played games, and shared his own experiences growing up in the area. Since many of them didn't have the money to attend movies, he purchased more than 300 tickets so they could see *Black Panther* in the theater when it came out.

Chadwick's impact extended beyond the world of cinema, touching the lives of many people. One of the ways he did that was by partnering with organizations like the Make-A-Wish Foundation, which fulfills the dreams of children who suffer from serious illnesses. A lot of them

yearned for an actual superhero encounter, so Chadwick would often surprise these brave kids by dressing up as Black Panther and bringing a little bit of Marvel Cinematic Universe magic into their lives. Imagine the joy and excitement on their faces as they met their hero, T'Challa, in person—a memory they would cherish forever.

One touching anecdote involved two young boys who were battling cancer in the months before *Black Panther* came out. In a SiriusXM interview, Chadwick shared how he spoke with

their parents during filming. "They're trying to hold on 'til this movie comes," they said, which made Chadwick work harder to make *Black Panther* even better.

Sadly, the boys passed away before the film's release, but Chadwick was deeply moved by their story, and it fueled his commitment to making a difference through his work.

During the COVID epidemic, Chadwick stepped up once again. He donated more than $4 million to purchase personal protective equipment (PPE) for hospitals that served Black communities. He publicly encouraged others to do the same, and many listened.

Chadwick also used his platform to raise awareness about important issues, like social justice and equality. He participated in peaceful protests and spoke out against racism and injustice, using his voice to uplift and inspire others. In a memorable 2018 speech at Howard University, his **alma mater**, Chadwick told the graduating class, "Purpose is the essential element of you. It is the reason you are on the planet at this particular time in history." His words continue to inspire young people to find their purpose and make a difference in the world.

Chadwick truly cared about making a positive impact on the lives of others. He understood the power of kindness, compassion, and the importance of using his platform for good. His actions off-screen were just as heroic as the characters he portrayed on-screen, and his legacy of giving back continues to inspire countless people around the world.

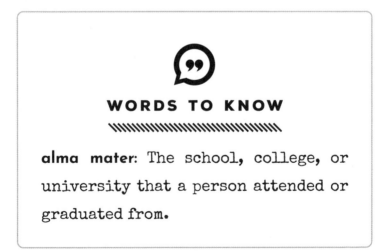

WORDS TO KNOW

alma mater: The school, college, or university that a person attended or graduated from.

THE WORLD AT THE TIME

In 2018:

- *Avengers: Infinity War* premieres in theaters, becoming a major blockbuster in the Marvel Cinematic Universe.
- Prince Harry and Meghan Markle get married in a highly publicized royal wedding.
- Childish Gambino's song "This is America" sparks conversation and goes viral with its thought-provoking music video.

WHAT DO YOU THINK?

- In what ways can other celebrities learn from Chadwick's life and legacy?

- During Chadwick's rise to fame as Black Panther, he was quietly dating singer Taylor Simone Ledward, who later became his wife. After Chadwick's passing, she helped launch the Chadwick Boseman Foundation for the Arts, which seeks to amplify and support the stories and voices of young Black creatives across America. How is that a fitting extension of Chadwick's own efforts?

9

The Ultimate Battle: Chadwick vs. Cancer, a True Warrior's Tale

What they don't realize is the greatest conflict you will ever face will be the conflict with yourself.

—CHADWICK BOSEMAN

It's time to talk about something a bit more serious.

We've seen our hero rise to stardom, inspire millions, and give back to the world. But did you know that Chadwick was secretly fighting a battle that would have knocked most people off their feet? Yes, our extraordinary hero was facing a villain more challenging than any he had ever encountered on-screen: cancer.

In 2016, Chadwick was diagnosed with colon cancer, a disease that affects the large intestine. Now, cancer is a tough opponent for anyone, but Chadwick was determined not to let it defeat him. He fought his battle in private, not wanting the world to focus on his illness, but rather on his work and the causes he cared about. He continued to act, inspire, and help others, all while going through seemingly endless surgeries and treatments. That's a level of bravery even the mightiest superhero would admire!

Imagine Chadwick on a film set, in the middle of an intense action scene. He's dressed as Black Panther, leaping and dodging as he takes on enemies. The camera rolls, capturing every breathtaking move. But what we don't see is that Chadwick is pushing through pain and exhaustion, never once letting it show on his face. His determination and **resilience** are truly awe-inspiring.

Even when the going got tough, Chadwick never lost his passion for acting and storytelling. In one interview, Chadwick shared, "When I

stand in front of a camera, I feel alive. I can't let anything stop me from doing what I love." He believed in the power of the arts to inspire and uplift, and he continued to bring incredible characters to life on-screen. And all the while, he was still making time to visit sick children, attend charity events, and lend his voice to important causes.

Chadwick's friends and colleagues have spoken about his astonishing strength during this time. Costar Michael B. Jordan said, "Chadwick was a true fighter. He persevered through it all and brought you many of the films you have come to love so much." It's a testament to Chadwick's character that he continued to create and inspire, even when squaring off against the formidable foe that is cancer.

So, what can we learn from Chadwick's secret health struggle? For one, it's essential to recognize that everyone is fighting their own battles, and it's crucial to be kind and supportive. We can also learn that even in the face of adversity, it's possible to keep pushing forward and make a difference in the world.

In August 2020, Chadwick sadly lost his battle with cancer, leaving the world heartbroken. But the amazing thing about our hero is that even though he's no longer with us, his spirit and legacy live on. Chadwick taught us that it's not about how much time we have on this earth, but what we do with that time.

As Chadwick himself once said, "You have to cherish things in a different way when you know the clock is ticking, you are under pressure." Let's take a moment to appreciate the incredible life and legacy of Chadwick Boseman, a true superhero on and off the screen.

WORDS TO KNOW

resilience: The ability to bounce back and keep going even after facing challenges or difficult situations.

THE WORLD AT THE TIME

In 2020:

- the COVID-19 pandemic affects the entire world, leading to lockdowns, remote learning, and mask wearing.
- SpaceX launches the Crew Dragon, the first private spacecraft to carry astronauts to the International Space Station.
- TikTok explodes in popularity.

WHAT DO YOU THINK?

- How did Chadwick's private struggle with cancer affect your perception of him?
- Since 2015, Chadwick and singer Taylor Simone Ledward had been dating. Few knew that in 2020, they quietly got married. Why do you think they kept their relationship out of the spotlight?

10

Forever Our Hero: The Unforgettable Legacy of Chadwick Boseman

Fearlessness means taking the first step, even if you don't know where it will take you. It means being driven by a higher purpose, rather than by applause. It means knowing that you reveal your character when you stand apart more than when you stand with the crowd.

—CHADWICK BOSEMAN

A nd now, we've reached the final chapter of our hero's epic journey. We've seen Chadwick's rise to stardom, his inspiring humanitarian work, and his courageous fight with cancer. But what about the legacy he left behind and the impact he has on future generations?

Chadwick's portrayal of T'Challa in *Black Panther* changed the game when it came to representation in media. He showed the world that heroes come in all shapes, sizes, and colors, and his performance opened the door for more diverse stories to be told. In a 2019 Screen Actors Guild Awards acceptance speech, Chadwick explained the challenges faced by young, gifted Black creatives, saying, "We know what it's like to be told there's not a screen for you to be featured on, a stage for you to be featured on. We know what it's like to be the tail and not the head. We know what it's like to be beneath and not above."

He made it his mission to change that narrative, and his impact on the industry is undeniable.

Imagine a young Black child sitting in a movie theater, eyes wide with wonder as they watch Black Panther on the big screen. They see T'Challa—a strong, intelligent, and compassionate hero—who looks like them, and suddenly, anything seems possible. That's the power of

representation, and it's a legacy Chadwick has left for generations to come.

But Chadwick's influence goes beyond the characters he brought to life on-screen. His humanitarian work and commitment to helping others have inspired countless people to follow in his footsteps. He taught us that success is about more than fame and fortune—it's about using our gifts to create a positive impact in our communities and throughout the world.

One example of his legacy is Howard University. After Chadwick lost his battle with cancer, the school honored his life and contribution by naming a building after him. As of September 2021, students can now follow in Chadwick's footsteps by attending the Chadwick A. Boseman College of Fine Arts. In a statement about that honor, Boseman's family said, "His time at Howard University helped shape both the man and the artist he became—committed to truth, **integrity**, and a determination to transform the world through the power of storytelling."

Will another *Black Panther* or Marvel Studios superhero movie feature a current or future Howard University student? The chances for that to happen just improved. A lot.

Celebrities and fans alike have spoken out about the lasting influence Chadwick has had on their lives.

"Chadwick came to the White House to work with kids when he was playing Jackie Robinson. You could tell right away that he was blessed. To be young, gifted, and Black; to use that power to give them heroes to look up to; to do it all while in pain—what a use of his years." —BARACK OBAMA

"Here's to an incredible man with immeasurable talent, who leaned into life regardless of his personal battles. You never truly know what the people around you might be going through—treat them with kindness and cherish every minute you have together." —HALLE BERRY

"This is a crushing blow." —JORDAN PEELE

"I've been trying to find the words, but nothing comes close to how I feel. I've been reflecting on every moment, every conversation, every laugh, every disagreement, every hug . . . everything. I wish we had more time." —MICHAEL B. JORDAN

"All I have to say is the tragedies amassing this year have only been made more profound by the loss of #ChadwickBoseman. What a man, and what an immense talent. Brother, you were one of the all-time greats, and your greatness was only beginning." —MARK RUFFALO

"I write these words from a place of hopelessness, to honor a man who had great hope. Chadwick was a man who made the most of his time and somehow also managed to take his time."

—LUPITA NYONG'O

"What a gentle gifted SOUL. Showing us all that Greatness in between surgeries and **chemo**. The courage, the strength, the Power it takes to do that. This is what **dignity** looks like."

—OPRAH WINFREY

"He was a gentle soul and a brilliant artist, who will stay with us for eternity through his iconic performances over his short yet **illustrious** career. God bless Chadwick Boseman."

—DENZEL WASHINGTON

"Chadwick Boseman was a beautiful spirit, a **consummate** artist, a soulful brother, a joy to work with, and a true friend. His talent was surpassed only by his character, his kindness, and his grace. Rest in Peace, Chadwick. You are deeply loved and will be missed." —PHYLICIA RASHAD

So, as we close the book on the incredible life and journey of Chadwick Boseman, let's remember the lessons he taught us—the power of storytelling, the importance of representation, and the astounding impact one person can have on the world. Chadwick may no longer be with us, but his spirit and legacy will live on forever in the hearts of those he touched.

Let's imagine Chadwick one more time, standing tall as T'Challa, looking out over the

stunning landscape of Wakanda. The sun is shining, and the wind gently rustles the leaves of the trees. He raises his hands in the iconic Wakanda salute, a smile on his face, as he watches over the people he loves and the world he helped create. He knows that his journey may have come to an end, but his story will live on, inspiring countless others to be heroes in their own right.

So, here's to you, Chadwick—thank you for being our hero, our inspiration, and our shining light. As T'Challa himself would say, "Wakanda Forever!"

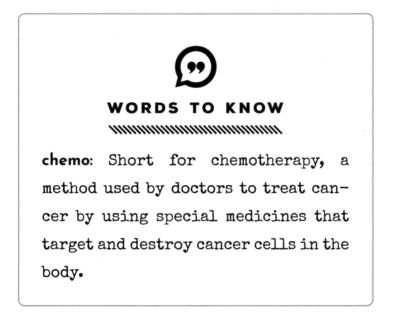

WORDS TO KNOW

chemo: Short for chemotherapy, a method used by doctors to treat cancer by using special medicines that target and destroy cancer cells in the body.

integrity: Being honest and doing the right thing, even when no one is watching or it's hard to do.

consummate: Having great skill, expertise, or talent in a particular area, making someone or something exceptionally good at what they do.

dignity: The feeling of being respected and valued, even when facing difficult situations.

illustrious: Used to describe someone who has an outstanding reputation and is known for their remarkable accomplishments; often leaving a lasting impact.

THE WORLD AT THE TIME

In 2020:

- The Weeknd's "Blinding Lights" is a chart-topping hit and inspires numerous TikTok dance challenges.

- the bestselling Christmas toy is the *Star Wars: The Mandalorian*—The Child (Baby Yoda) plush toy.
- the most successful video-on-demand release is *Trolls World Tour*, which earned over $100 million in rental revenue in its first three weeks.

WHAT DO YOU THINK?

- How do you think Chadwick would like to be remembered by his fans and the world?
- With *Black Panther 2: Wakanda Forever*, the decision was made not to recast the character or reproduce him with CGI. If that choice was yours to make, how would you have handled it?

Glossary

Afrofuturistic—A cultural and artistic movement that combines African history, traditions, and futuristic elements; often in science fiction and fantasy works.

alma mater—The school, college, or university that a person attended or graduated from.

biopic—A movie that tells the story of someone's life, usually about a famous or important person.

bonafide—Genuine, authentic, or legitimate; often used to describe something or someone that is real, sincere, or truly qualified, without any deception or doubt.

change agent—Someone who helps make big, positive changes happen, often by inspiring or leading others.

chemo—Short for chemotherapy, a method used by doctors to treat cancer by using special medicines that target and destroy cancer cells in the body.

consummate—Having great skill, expertise, or talent in a particular area, making someone or something exceptionally good at what they do.

dignity—The feeling of being respected and valued, even when facing difficult situations.

Emmy—An award given annually for outstanding achievements in television, recognizing excellence in acting, directing, writing, and more.

formidable—Something or someone that is very powerful and impressive, making it hard to compete with or overcome.

Harlem Renaissance—A time in the 1920s and 1930s when African American artists, writers, and musicians created lots of amazing new art, music, and literature in a neighbor-hood called Harlem in New York City.

honed—To make something, like a skill or talent, better and sharper through lots of hard practice or work.

humanitarian—A person who is dedicated to improving the lives of others, often through actions such as providing aid and support or advocating for human rights.

illustrious—Used to describe someone who has an outstanding reputation and is known for their remarkable accomplishments; often leaving a lasting impact.

indelible—Something that cannot be erased or removed; often referring to a lasting memory, impression, or mark.

integrity—Being honest and doing the right thing, even when no one is watching or it's hard to do.

jazz era (Jazz Age)—A time during the 1920s when jazz music was very popular and people loved to dance and have fun.

Jim Crow—A term referring to the racist laws and policies in the United States that enforced racial segregation and limited the rights of African Americans, mostly in the South, from the late 1800s to the mid-1900s.

Mecca—A place that attracts a specific group of people due to its importance or significance, often used figuratively; also, the holiest city in Islam, located in Saudi Arabia.

NAACP—The National Association for the Advancement of Colored People, a civil rights organization founded in 1909 to fight for the rights and equality of African Americans in the United States.

nuance—A subtle difference or distinction in meaning, opinion, or expression; often requiring careful attention to understand or appreciate fully.

Oscar—An award given annually for outstanding achievements in the film industry, recognizing excellence in acting, directing, writing, and more, presented by the Academy of Motion Picture Arts and Sciences.

palpable—Something that is so strong or clear that you can almost feel or touch it, like the excitement in a room before a big event.

philanthropy—The act of giving time, money, or help to others, especially to make the world a better place.

posthumous—Something that occurs or is awarded after a person's death, such as a book being published or an award being given.

resilience—The ability to bounce back and keep going even after facing challenges or difficult situations.

salute—A gesture of respect, usually done by raising a hand to the forehead.

segregation—The practice of separating people based on factors such as race, gender, or religion; often used to discuss the forced separation of different racial groups.

Tony—An award given annually for outstanding achievements in live Broadway theater, recognizing excellence in acting, directing, writing, and more.

vegan—A person who does not eat or use animal products, including meat, dairy, eggs, and sometimes even honey; often for ethical, health, or environmental reasons.

Timeline

1976: Born in Anderson, South Carolina.

2000: Graduated from Howard University (Washington, DC) with a degree in directing

2001: Graduated from New York City's Digital Film Academy

2008: Landed first professional acting role on the daytime TV soap opera *All My Children*

2008: Got first continuing role on a TV show with *Lincoln Heights*

2008: Acted in his first movie, *The Express*

2013: Starred as Jackie Robinson in the film *42*

2014: Starred as James Brown in the film *Get On Up*

2016: Starred as Black Panther in *Captain America: Civil War*

2017: Starred as Thurgood Marshall in the film *Marshall*

2018: Starred as King T'Challa in the film *Black Panther*

2018: Served as Commencement Speaker at Howard University

2020: Quietly married his longtime partner, singer Taylor Simone Ledward

2020: Starred in the last film to be released in his lifetime, *Da 5 Bloods*

2020: Passed away from colon cancer at age 43 on August 28

2020: Chadwick's final film, *Ma Rainey's Black Bottom*, was released by Netflix after Chadwick's death

Selected Bibliography

Eels, Josh. "The 'Black Panther' Revolution. *Rolling Stone*. 17 February 2018.

Johnson, Lauren. "Howard University alum Chadwick Boseman's Powerful Commencement Speech Challenged Students and Praised Protestors." CNN.com, 29 August 2020.

Johnson, Mia. *Chadwick Boseman: Forever Our King, 1976-2020*. Triumph Books, 2020.

Narcisse, Evan. "Chadwick Boseman Was Ready for History Every Time." *GQ*, 1 September 2020.

Pope-Johns, Imani. "Howard Forever: The Impact of Chadwick Boseman Beyond Howard University." *Howard Magazine*, Spring 2021.

Rose, Tony and Yvonne Rose. *Journey to Wakanda Black Panther & Beyond . . . The Life and Legacy of Chadwick Boseman.* Colossus Books, 2022.

Uwu, Reggie and Michael Levenson. "'Black Panther' Star Chadwick Boseman Dies of Cancer at 43.'" *New York Times*. 28 August 2020.

About Chris Singleton

Chris Singleton is a former professional athlete drafted by the Chicago Cubs in 2017. Following the loss of his mother in a racially motivated mass shooting, Chris has now become an inspirational speaker and bestselling author who has shared his message of unity and racial reconciliation with NFL and NBA teams as well as multiple Fortune 500 companies across the country. He shares with over 100 organizations and over 30,000 students annually. He resides with his spouse, Mariana, and three children in Charleston, South Carolina.

About Ryan G. Van Cleave

Dr. Ryan G. Van Cleave is the author of dozens of fiction, nonfiction, and poetry books for both children and adults. When Ryan's not writing, he's crisscrossing the country, teaching writing at schools throughout the United States. He also moonlights as The Picture Book Whisperer™, helping celebrities write stories for kids and bring them to life on the page, stage, and screen.

Adriana Pérez Perales

Adriana is a freelance illustrator from Mexico. Her clients include Oxford University Press, Scholastic, Get Ready Comics, and many others.

MILK +
COOKIES

About Milk & Cookies

Milk & Cookies is the middle-grade imprint of Bushel & Peck Books, a children's publisher with a special mission. Through our Book-for-Book Promise™, we donate one book to kids in need for every book we sell. Our beautiful books are given to kids through schools, libraries, local neighborhoods, shelters, and nonprofits, and also to many selfless organizations that are working hard to make a difference. So thank you for purchasing this book! Because of you, another book will make its way into the hands of a child who needs it most. Do you know a school, a library, or an organization that could use some free books for their kids? We'd love to help! Please fill out the nomination form on our website, and we'll do everything we can to make something happen.